The Fourth Street Garage Band

by Barbara A. Donovan

illustrated by Jeremy Tugeau

Harcourt
SCHOOL PUBLISHERS

Requests for permission to make copies of any part of the work should be addressed to School Permissions and Copyrights, Harcourt, Inc., 6277 Sea Harbor Drive, Orlando, Florida 32887-6777. Fax: 407-345-2418.

HARCOURT and the Harcourt Logo are trademarks of Harcourt, Inc., registered in the United States of America and/or other jurisdictions.

Printed in China

ISBN 10: 0-15-350301-7
ISBN 13: 978-0-15-350301-6

Ordering Options
ISBN 10: 0-15-349941-9 (Grade 6 ELL Collection)
ISBN 13: 978-0-15-349941-8 (Grade 6 ELL Collection)
ISBN 10: 0-15-357341-4 (package of 5)
ISBN 13: 978-0-15-357341-5 (package of 5)

5 6 7 8 9 10   0940   15 14 13 12 11 10 09

Today turned out to be the most fantastic day of my life! I woke up this morning feeling very happy. I was so excited! Today is Saturday.

Anthony, Dylan, J.J. and I are friends. We have a band called "Fourth Street Garage." The band is named after my garage. That is where we practice. We practice every Saturday morning. Today "Fourth Street Garage" is going to make a video to enter in a school contest.

We hope the judges will like our video best. Then we might get to make a video for our school's Web site. Everybody who visited the Web site would be able to see and hear us play. We would be famous!

This Saturday we met very early in the morning for one last practice. We wanted to practice before we made the tape.

Anthony, Dylan, J.J. and I practiced for two hours. Then we all felt that we were finally ready to set up the video camera and record our performance. Anthony had borrowed his dad's video camera and the stand that went with it. The stand had three legs. One leg was broken, so the camera kept tipping over. We taped the leg. Then we stuffed some magazines under it. That way, it would stay in place. At last, we were ready.

Dylan, J.J., and I took our places. Then Anthony pressed the start button on the camera. He ran back to his place. However, Anthony's microphone must have moved by accident. When he stood in front of the microphone to play his electric guitar, he knocked the speakers over. Anthony turned them off. Then we adjusted the speakers. We took our places once again. Then Anthony started the camera, and we taped our whole performance.

We went inside my house when we were done. We connected the video camera to the television set. Then we sat down to watch our performance. We were surprised to see that there was no picture on the television. It must have been too dark in the garage. You could hear us, but you couldn't see us.

We were very disappointed. Anthony looked so sad. We sounded as good as we ever had. However, we were going to have to record the performance all over again.

My mom let us take some lamps from the house to the garage. We plugged them in and turned them on. The lamps gave us plenty of light. Then we took our places. Anthony turned on the video camera and ran to his place.

When Anthony strummed the first notes on his guitar, all the lights in the garage went out! We could not believe the lights went out!

I was so upset. It was unbelievable that so many things could go wrong. We must have used too many lights. We had blown a fuse in the garage. Mom fixed it for us. Then she shut off some lights so that we wouldn't blow another fuse.

We got ready again. We tested our instruments. The lights didn't go out when we started playing this time. We checked that the stand for the video camera was set. Everything seemed right at last. Anthony pressed the button to start the camera. He ran back to his place, and we began playing.

Our band had never sounded so good. We were all feeling fantastic as we finished and shut off the camera. We were great! We hooked up the video camera to the TV in the house. We were thrilled with how we looked on the screen. The "Fourth Street Garage" sounded great.

Then Dylan said, "Do you hear a strange noise in the background?" We backed the video up and listened closely.

"It's Shadow," I said. The dog next door was howling all through our song. The noise was not loud, but we could hear it. Dylan and J.J. wanted to enter the video into the contest as it was. Anthony and I thought we were sure to lose with the dog howling in the background. Then I had an idea.

I looked through the refrigerator. I was searching for something to give Shadow that would keep him busy. Foods like carrots and celery wouldn't work for long.

Then I had an idea. I asked my mom whether I could give Shadow one of the soup bones from the freezer. Mom said it was okay as long as Mr. Jenkins, Shadow's owner, agreed.

Mr. Jenkins agreed that I could give Shadow the bone. Then we had peace and quiet. The band members took their places one last time. We knew we had to get it right this time. We had to deliver the video to the school by four o'clock.

Anthony started the video camera once again. He ran back and took his place, and we began playing. This time, when we finished, we knew we had played well. However, we wondered what disaster we would discover when we played back the video.

We each held our breath as the video began to play. We couldn't believe our eyes and ears. Nothing went wrong! The Fourth Street Garage video was fantastic!

Now we just had to deliver it to school. We were afraid that something else might go wrong on the way, but we made it there without a problem. We handed the tape over just in time.

Does our act deserve to win? I know it does. We surely tried just as hard as anyone else in this contest. We shall see.

Scaffolded Language Development

PREFIXES AND SUFFIXES Write the following sentence from the story on the board: *It was unbelievable that so many things could go wrong.* Point out the word *unbelievable,* and tell students that some words can have both a prefix and a suffix. Remind students that sometimes the spelling of the root word changes before the suffix can be added. Have students identify the root word *believe,* the prefix-*un,* and the suffix-*able.* Help students determine the meaning of the word ("not to be believed").

Have students follow a similar procedure using the following words:

unavoidable	untamable
undeniable	unburnable
unlikable	unpredictable

 **Social Studies**

Research Ask students to research Thomas Edison and find out about his role in developing the motion picture camera. How did his discoveries affect the way people watched movies? Have students share their information with the group.

School-Home Connection

Planning Events Have students tell family members about the troubles the band had in the story. Suggest that they discuss times in their lives when things didn't go as planned.

Word Count: 928